Searchlight
BOOKS™

What
Are Energy
Sources?

Finding Out about

Geothermal

Energy

Matt Doeden

Lerner Publications Company
Minneapolis

Lerner Publications Company
A division of Lerner Publishing Group, Inc.
241 First Avenue North
Minneapolis, MN 55401 USA

For reading levels and more information, look up this title at www.lernerbooks.com.

Library of Congress Cataloging-in-Publication Data

Doeden, Matt.
    Finding out about geothermal energy / by Matt Doeden.
        pages   cm. — (Searchlight books™—What are energy sources?)
    Includes index.
    ISBN 978-1-4677-3658-9 (lib. bdg. : alk. paper)
    ISBN 978-1-4677-4638-0 (eBook)
    1. Geothermal engineering—Juvenile literature. 2. Geothermal resources—Juvenile literature. I. Title.
    TJ280.7.D66 2015
    621.44—dc23   2013036369

Manufactured in the United States of America
1 — BP — 7/15/14

Contents

Chapter 1

WHAT IS GEOTHERMAL ENERGY?

Imagine digging a hole hundreds or thousands of feet beneath Earth's surface. What would you find? The ground might seem cool as you dig a few feet down. But that soon changes. You dig deeper, and it gets warmer. And warmer. And *warmer*! Soon it's hotter than you can stand.

The ground is cool when you first dig into it. Does it stay cool as you dig deeper?

Why is this? Earth has a lot of heat inside it. And the farther down you go, the hotter it gets. The heat trapped deep inside Earth is called geothermal energy. *Geo* means "earth." *Thermal* means "heat."

Earth's heat warms these waters in Yellowstone National Park.

Geothermal energy has two main uses. It can heat buildings. Or it can be used to make electricity. We usually just have to dig a little to reach it.

In some areas of the world, you can swim in water heated by geothermal energy.

Where Does Geothermal Energy Come From?

Earth's center is called the core. Temperatures there can reach 9,000°F (5,000°C). That is hot enough to melt rock! But where does all that heat come from?

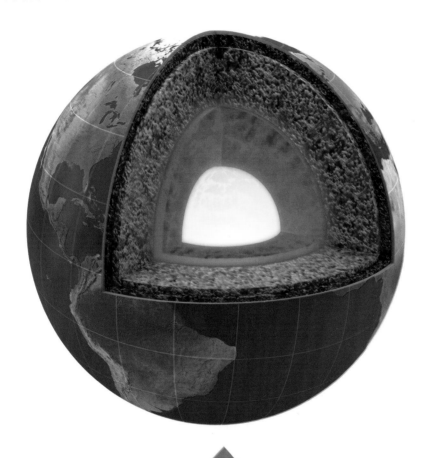

EARTH HAS FOUR LAYERS. THE CENTER LAYER IS THE INNER CORE.

Some of the heat is left over from when Earth formed. That happened about 4 billion years ago. Earth formed as dust and gas collapsed together. The collapse created a lot of heat.

The heat from when Earth was formed plays an important role in geothermal energy today.

When magma erupts out of a volcano, it is called lava.

Much of the heat was trapped deep inside Earth. It was so hot that rocks melted into a liquid called magma. Some of that heat remains inside Earth to this day. About 20 percent of the core's heat is left over from when Earth formed.

Most of the remaining 80 percent is created by radioactive decay. This is the process by which some materials decay, or break down, over time. Atoms are the basic building blocks of matter. Some types of atoms are radioactive. They break down. When they do, they release a lot of energy. This energy becomes heat.

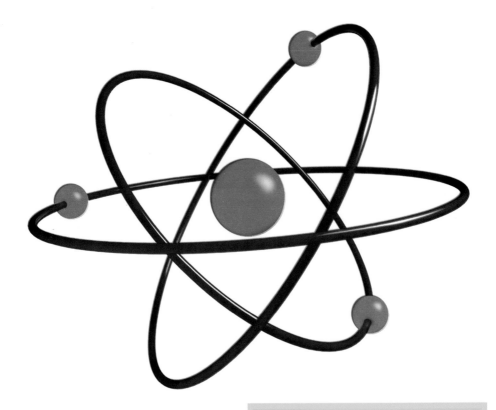

Atoms can release energy that becomes heat.

Pressure builds as water heats up. When pressure gets too high, water erupts from the surface.

But the heat doesn't just stay in the core. The hotter magma is, the lighter it is. So it slowly flows outward, toward the surface. It carries some of the core's heat with it. This keeps everything underground warm. When we tap into this heat, we can get energy.

Chapter 2

COLLECTING GEOTHERMAL ENERGY

People have used geothermal energy for thousands of years. In some places, hot springs reach the surface. These pools of water are heated by Earth. People in places such as ancient China and ancient Rome used these hot springs as baths. Some even used the water to heat their homes.

Ancient people used water heated by geothermal energy to bathe. What was another way that ancient people used these warm waters?

Simple heating systems such as these still exist. Iceland has many hot springs. Pipes carry the hot water into homes. The water gives off its heat and keeps the homes warm. It is a very easy and cheap way to stay warm. But most parts of the world are far from hot springs. Using Earth's heat in these places is a little trickier.

Pipes can carry heat from hot springs to homes.

Workers install a geothermal heat pump.

Geothermal Heat Pumps

You probably don't have a hot spring in your backyard. That means that you'll have to dig to get at Earth's heat. And many homeowners are doing just that. They are putting geothermal heat pumps (GHPs) into their homes.

The first step is to dig and bury a long loop of pipe. It is usually placed 10 to 300 feet (3 to 90 meters) deep. The pipe is filled with water or other fluids. A pump sends the water underground. The warm ground heats it.

Pipes for geothermal heat pumps carry water underground.

The water is pumped back to the surface. The heat it carries is used to warm the home. Some GHPs use the water to heat air. Others pump it to a series of pipes under the floor. Either way, the water's heat spreads out in the home. The cooled water then goes back underground to get more heat.

This machine is part of a geothermal heat pump system. The machine pumps the water.

Heat pumps even help cool homes in the summer. The pumps take warmth out of the air. The pumps send the warm water underground. There, it cools. Then it returns to the surface to do it all over again.

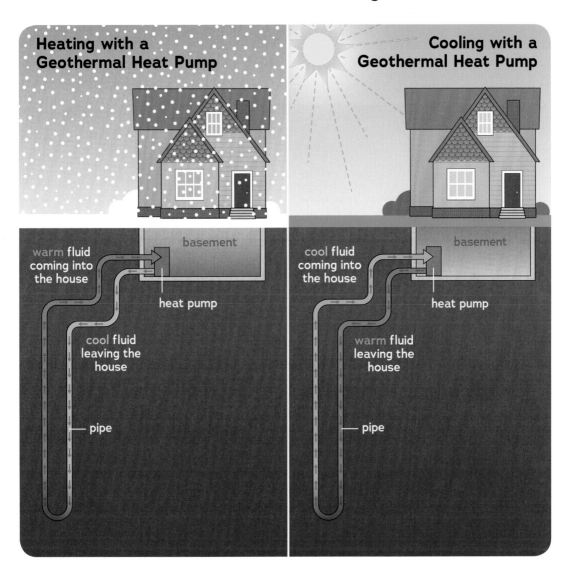

Heating with a Geothermal Heat Pump

basement

warm **fluid** coming into the house

heat pump

cool **fluid** leaving the house

pipe

Cooling with a Geothermal Heat Pump

basement

cool **fluid** coming into the house

heat pump

warm **fluid** leaving the house

pipe

Geothermal Electricity

We can also use Earth's heat to make electricity. That's the job of geothermal power plants. These power plants need a lot of heat to work. Workers usually have to drill 1 mile (1.6 kilometers) or deeper to find a spot that is hot enough.

GEOTHERMAL ENERGY CAN ALSO BE USED TO PRODUCE ELECTRICITY.

The flash steam power plant is the most common kind. These plants work anywhere that underground water reaches at least 360°F (182°C). This superhot water is pumped to the surface.

This is a flash steam power plant.

Generators such as these turn energy from steam into electricity.

The hot water is released into an area where the air pressure is very low. In low air pressure, water turns to steam much more easily. So as the water enters the area of low pressure, some of it instantly flashes into steam. The steam rises and turns turbines. Then machines turn the steam's energy into electricity.

What about where water is cooler? That makes the job harder. But it can still be done. Binary cycle power plants use water that isn't hot enough to flash to steam. They use the warm water to heat other liquids such as isobutane. Isobutane turns to a vapor at a lower temperature than water. The vapor powers the turbine.

In binary cycle power plants, vapor powers a turbine that generates electricity.

What if there's no water underground at all? Can we get electricity then? Yes! The process starts with a deep well. The well is dug 2 to 6 miles (3.2 to 9.7 km) deep. Water is pumped down into the well. Earth heats the water. The hot water is pumped back up. There, it works just like a binary plant.

Some geothermal power plants rely on deep wells dug in the ground.

Chapter 3

THE PROS AND CONS OF GEOTHERMAL ENERGY

Many people believe geothermal energy is a key part of our energy future. Fossil fuels such as coal, oil, and natural gas provide most of the world's power. But these energy sources are nonrenewable. This means once they are gone, they are gone for good.

This coal is a nonrenewable energy source. What does *nonrenewable* mean?

Geothermal energy is renewable. Earth will continue to create heat for billions of years. We may be limited by how much energy we can collect. But we won't run out of it.

Geothermal energy is renewable. That means Earth won't run out of it.

The Cost of Geothermal Energy

Geothermal energy is mostly clean. It is also reliable. So why isn't it everywhere? One simple reason—installing a GHP is expensive. Putting a GHP into a home can cost from $10,000 to $25,000. And you still need electricity to run the pump.

The high startup cost of geothermal heat pumps prevents most families from installing them.

But over time, energy savings can really add up. A GHP can reduce energy costs by 40 percent or more. Over decades, the pumps can save homeowners money.

Once they are in place, geothermal energy systems can save families money on heating and cooling their homes.

Geothermal power plants release steam that doesn't hurt the environment.

The Environment

Most forms of geothermal energy are friendly to the environment. The water needed for the pumps isn't used up. It can be reused again and again. Or it can be boiled off as harmless steam.

Many people are worried about climate change. This is the process by which Earth's global climate changes over a period of time. Earth is getting warmer, and it is warming faster than it has in a long time.

Pollution from cars contributes to climate change. Riding a bike instead of driving cuts down on pollution.

This is because people are adding heat-trapping gases into the atmosphere. These include carbon dioxide. Burning fossil fuels releases tons of carbon dioxide.

MOST VEHICLES RELEASE CARBON DIOXIDE THAT POLLUTES THE AIR.

Scientists warn that too much change too fast could be a disaster. So people are searching for energy sources that don't give off carbon dioxide. Collecting Earth's heat doesn't release any. That makes geothermal energy a great choice.

Solar panels are another Earth-friendly way of bringing energy to a home.

Still, geothermal energy isn't completely safe. Some underground water contains toxins such as mercury. Power plants that aren't careful can leak these toxins onto Earth's surface. The toxins can get into water supplies. That is harmful to people and animals who use the water.

Animals rely on clean water to survive.

Deeper Impacts

Certain types of geothermal power plants create problems deep beneath the surface. Pumping water underground can cause small earthquakes.

Pumping water underground can cause earthquakes that damage roads.

In some places, geothermal plants have caused the land to sink. The removal of water underground causes small cracks to form in the rock. The cracks can collapse. Everything above the collapsed rock then sinks. This is called subsidence. Land may sink only a few inches or feet. That may not sound like a lot. But it's enough to damage roads, pipes, and buildings.

Damage such as this can cost lots of money.

Still, most experts agree that the benefits of geothermal energy outweigh the costs. It's a clean, reliable, and renewable energy source. We can use it while doing very little damage to Earth.

GEOTHERMAL ENERGY CAN BE USED TO MAKE ELECTRICITY TWENTY-FOUR HOURS A DAY.

Chapter 4

GEOTHERMAL ENERGY IN THE FUTURE

The fossil fuels we are using won't last forever. And scientists are learning that continuing to burn fossil fuels could cause terrible damage to Earth's climate, environment, and living things. Problems stemming from burning fossil fuels include increased droughts and floods. These conditions could affect crops and food supplies. So the search for alternative energy sources is on.

Burning fossil fuels affects Earth in many ways. What is one way that burning these fuels affects our planet?

One Piece of the Puzzle

Geothermal energy can never fully meet all the world's energy needs. You can't pour geothermal energy into the fuel tank of a car, a bus, or an airplane. And the amount of electricity that we can generate from it is limited. Overusing a geothermal resource can cause it to cool. Power plants must be careful not to take out too much heat too quickly.

Gasoline is an energy source that pollutes the air and is nonrenewable.

Geothermal energy may not be the entire key to clean energy. But it could be a big part. Using it to heat and cool homes could reduce our need for coal and natural gas. Other alternative energy sources such as solar, wind, hydropower, and nuclear each have their own strengths. Currently, none of them can replace fossil fuels alone. But together, they could provide much of the power the world will need in the future.

WIND IS ANOTHER RENEWABLE ENERGY SOURCE. THESE WIND TURBINES GENERATE ELECTRICITY WITHOUT POLLUTING THE AIR.

Glossary

alternative energy source: a source of energy other than traditional fossil fuels

atom: the smallest unit of an element that has the properties of the element. An atom is made up of protons, neutrons, and electrons.

core: the very hot center of Earth

fossil fuel: a fuel such as coal, natural gas, or oil that was formed over millions of years from the remains of dead plants and animals

hot spring: a place where water heated by Earth reaches the surface

magma: hot, liquid rock beneath Earth's surface

nonrenewable: not able to be replenished. Once a nonrenewable form of energy is gone, it is used up for good.

radioactive decay: when certain elements break down, releasing energy as heat

reliable: able to be depended upon

renewable: able to be replenished over time

subsidence: when land slowly sinks

toxin: a substance that is poisonous to people and animals

turbine: a machine with blades that converts the energy from a moving fluid or gas, such as steam, into mechanical energy

vapor: a substance that is normally a liquid or a solid that is suspended in the air, such as steam

LERNER

SOURCE™

Expand learning beyond the printed book. Download free, complementary educational resources for this book from our website, www.lerneresource.com.

Learn More about Geothermal Energy

Books

Bailey, Gerry. *Out of Energy.* New York: Gareth Stevens, 2011. Learn more about alternatives to fossil fuels, from geothermal to solar, and find out how you can use energy more efficiently.

Doeden, Matt. *Finding Out about Coal, Oil, and Natural Gas.* Minneapolis: Lerner Publications, 2015. Fossil fuels remain our main source of energy. Learn more about how they form, how they're collected, and the pros and cons of using them.

Wachtel, Alan. *Geothermal Energy.* New York: Chelsea Clubhouse, 2010. Explore the history of geothermal energy and learn why many scientists believe it is one of the cleanest energy sources available.

Walker, Sally M. *Investigating Heat.* Minneapolis: Lerner Publications, 2012. Geothermal energy comes from heat. In this book, learn more about what heat is, what creates it, and how it affects the world.

Websites

Energy Kids—Geothermal
http://www.eia.gov/kids/energy.cfm?page=geothermal_home-basics
The US Energy Information Administration's page on geothermal energy includes diagrams and maps that will teach you more about geothermal energy.

How Geothermal Energy Works
http://science.howstuffworks.com/environmental/energy/geothermal-energy.htm
Check out a detailed description of geothermal energy and the ways we can collect it.

A Student's Guide to Global Climate Change—Geothermal Energy
http://www.epa.gov/climatestudents/solutions/technologies/geothermal.html
At this US Environmental Protection Agency site, read more about how geothermal heat pumps and power plants work.

Index

Photo Acknowledgments

The images in this book are used with the permission of: © Catalin Petolea/Dreamstime.com, p. 4; © iStockphoto.com/elgol, p. 5; © Buurserstraat386/Dreamstime.com, p. 6; © iStockphoto.com/adventtr, p. 7; © Stocktrek Images/Getty Images, p. 8; U.S. Geological Survey/photo by J.D. Griggs, p. 9; © Leigh Prather/Dreamstime.com, p. 10; © iStockphoto.com/Videowok_art, p. 11; © DeAgostini/SuperStock, p. 12; © iStockphoto.com/Rhoberazzi, pp. 13, 27; John Barlean/Department of Energy/National Renewable Energy Laboratory, p. 14; Robert R. Jones/Department of Energy/National Renewable Energy Laboratory, p. 15; © iStockphoto.com/BanksPhotos, p. 16; © Laura Westlund/Independent Picture Service, p. 17; © Poznukhov Yuriy/Shutterstock.com, p. 18; Warren Gretz/Department of Energy/National Renewable Energy Laboratory, p. 19; © Roger Asbury/Shutterstock.com, p. 20; © sergioboccardo/Shutterstock.com, p. 20; Robb Williamson/Department of Energy/National Renewable Energy Laboratory, p. 21; © Pancaketom/Dreamstime.com, p. 23; NASA/JPL, p. 24; © iStockphoto.com/bezov, p. 25; © Compassionate Eye Foundation/Digital Vision/Getty Images, p. 26; © spotmatik/Shutterstock.com, p. 28; © PhotoDisc Royalty Free by Getty Images, pp. 29, 37; © iStockphoto.com/chandlerphoto, p. 30; © iStockphoto.com/IJdema, p. 31; © Nigel Spiers/Dreamstime.com, p. 32; © Gerardo Mora/Getty Images News/Getty Images, p. 33; © Stephen Simpson/Taxi/Getty Images, p. 34; © iStockphoto.com/no_limit_pictures, p. 35; © iStockphoto.com/francisblack, p. 36.

Front cover: © Danielle Carnito.

Main body text set in Adrianna Regular 14/20
Typeface provided by Chank